EXTRA! EXTRA!

The Who, What, Where, When and Why of Newspapers

Written by LINDA GRANFIELD

Illustrated by BILL SLAVIN

Orchard Books
New York

Orchard Books
95 Madison Avenue
New York, NY 10016

Manufactured in the United States of America
Book design by Esperança Melo

10 9 8 7 6 5 4 3 2 1

The text of this book is set in Times, Garamond and
Franklin Gothic.
The illustrations are pencil on vellum.

Library of Congress Cataloging-in-Publication Data
Granfield, Linda.
  Extra! Extra! : the who, what, where, when and why of
newspapers / written by Linda Granfield ; illustrated by
Bill Slavin.
    p. cm.
  Originally published: Toronto : Kids Can Press.
  Includes index.
  ISBN 0-531-08683-6 (lib. bdg.) ISBN 0-531-07049-2 (pbk.)
  1. Newspapers — Juvenile literature. [1. Newspapers.]
  I. Slavin, Bill, ill. II. Title.
  PN4776.G73 1994 071'.3—dc20 93-11807

For my father, Joseph Granfield,
with much love and many thanks

ACKNOWLEDGMENTS

While researching a nonfiction title, one feels like a treasure-seeker, uncovering invaluable bits of glitter (and coal too) in books, pamphlets and, indeed, newspapers. This book is the result of a search brightened by witty stories from newsboys past and present, strangers encountered who "just happened to have a family member ... " and outright serendipity.

I am greatly indebted to Wilf Slater, Editorial Production Coordinator of the *Globe and Mail* (Canada), who gave me an author's dream tour of the entire *Globe* operation, answered oft-repeated questions with patience and humor and kindly (but with a critical eye) read the manuscript. Lynn Johnston generously shared her insights and cartoonist's talents one beautiful spring morning in northern Ontario. And others aided and abetted as well: Nickie Bonner and Robert Crooke of Reuters News Agency (Canada and U.S.); the Canadian Daily Newspaper Publishers Association; Selma M. Curtis, The Paper House (Massachusetts); Etobicoke (Ontario) Public Libraries; Camilla Gryski; R. Robert Herringer, the *Windsor Star* (Ontario); François Baby House: Windsor's Community Museum; the Kingston (Ontario) *Whig-Standard;* the staff of Mackenzie House, Toronto Historical Board; Bob Mayor, printer at Black Creek Pioneer Village (Ontario); Peg Schneider at the Tennessee State Museum; the *Toronto Sun;* the staff of Universal Press Syndicate (Missouri); Alan Walker of the Baldwin Room, Metropolitan Toronto Reference Library; and Gwen Wharton of the *Boston Globe.*

Many thanks to Kids Can Press, especially Lori Burwash, who attended to a myriad of production details; to Louise Oborne for her insights; to Bill Slavin and Esperança Melo for the wonderful illustrations and book design; to Cal, Devon and Brian Smiley, who provide an abundance of love and support; and especially to my editor, Val Wyatt, who continues to help me hone my writing skills — and keeps smiling all the while!

TABLE OF CONTENTS

INTRODUCTION

WHAT's black and white and read all over? Everyone knows the answer to this old joke — a newspaper.

But do you know what a newspaper has in common with a snapshot? Both capture a piece of the past. Every part of a newspaper is carefully planned to reflect what is going on in a community and in the world. A newspaper is a snapshot of our times, a time capsule of our history.

Since ancient times people have recorded important events.

• Cave people drew pictures on the walls of their caves. These illustrations are thought to record important happenings. Other news was passed along by word of mouth.

• Ancient Romans had one of the first newspapers in the world. Instead of being delivered door to door, it was posted each day in a public place. It told readers what was happening around the huge Roman Empire.

• The first American newspaper appeared on September 25, l690. This paper wasn't like today's newsy papers — it was just three pages of government information and news. And it came out only once because its publisher didn't have a license to print it.

• In 1704, postmaster John Campbell of Boston, Massachusetts, wrote the news in letters to his friends and sent it through the mail. More people wanted to read the news and were willing to pay for it. To avoid writer's cramp, Campbell began printing the news — and another newspaper was born!

• Until the 1800s, the only way to get a newspaper was with a subscription. Only the wealthy could afford a newspaper subscription. Then came newspapers called the "penny press," and ordinary people could afford to buy a newspaper.

Today, there are thousands of newspapers in many languages and in all shapes and sizes. You can read newspapers that specialize in stories about the fashion world, financial topics, even gossip. "Have you heard the latest…?"

It takes many people to record the news. Each person has a specific job to do in order to make a newspaper responsible and informative. Ready to find out about the people behind a daily newspaper? Meet the folks at the *Clairville Chronicle.*

1. Gathering the news

Open a newspaper and you'll find stories covering everything from politics to polo to pizza toppings. Where do all those stories come from and how do they get there? Turn the page to find out.

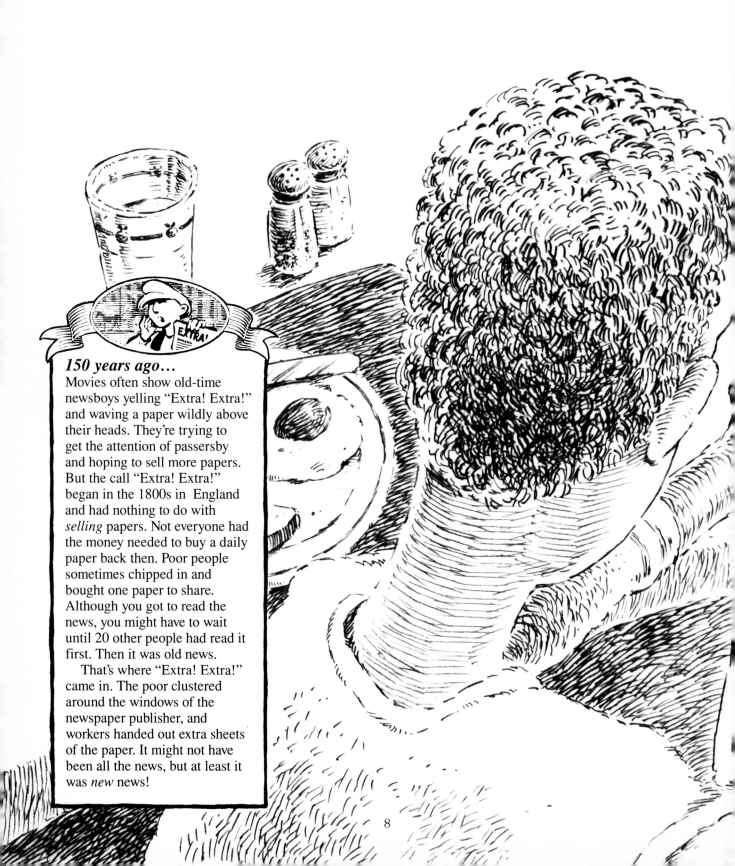

150 years ago…

Movies often show old-time newsboys yelling "Extra! Extra!" and waving a paper wildly above their heads. They're trying to get the attention of passersby and hoping to sell more papers. But the call "Extra! Extra!" began in the 1800s in England and had nothing to do with *selling* papers. Not everyone had the money needed to buy a daily paper back then. Poor people sometimes chipped in and bought one paper to share. Although you got to read the news, you might have to wait until 20 other people had read it first. Then it was old news.

That's where "Extra! Extra!" came in. The poor clustered around the windows of the newspaper publisher, and workers handed out extra sheets of the paper. It might not have been all the news, but at least it was *new* news!

Fire destroys local landmark

by **Rosie Longo**
CLAIRVILLE CHRONICLE

Throughout the night firefighters battled a blaze at the Morgan Pickle Factory on Prince Street. The factory, built by Thomas Morgan in 1793, was completely destroyed.

As flames licked out of the windows of the factory, neighbors gathered in the street.

"It's a shame," said Millie Taggart, who lives next door. "Those pickles were famous around the world."

Todd Ling, who reported the fire at 11 p.m., choked back tears. "I worked here as a boy. My father and grandfather worked here, too. It looks like the end of a long tradition."

No injuries were reported, and inspectors are sifting through the ashes. Although Fire Chief Sam Flame refused to comment on the cause of the blaze, a pile of paper and rags was found behind the factory. The fire marshall has ordered an investigation.

How did the *Clairville Chronicle* get the story?

When Todd Ling saw flames flickering inside the factory's windows, he dialed 911 and fire engines responded to the call. The

Chronicle, like many newspapers, monitors fire and police department calls. The *Chronicle's* editor called reporter Rosie Longo and assigned her to the story.

Rosie was curled up on her couch at home, enjoying a video and eating pizza (with anchovies) when the call came in. She would have to finish the pizza later.

Why Rosie? Some reporters have beats (special areas), such as the environment, city politics or sports. They become experts on their beats. The editor assigned Rosie because her beat is downtown business. Rosie already knew a lot about the pickle factory and the neighborhood, so she could file (turn in) her story quickly, in time to meet the final edition's deadline.

Smoke billowed out of the pickle factory as Rosie arrived. Hoses tripped her and water had started to freeze on the pavement. It was slippery underfoot, and Rosie had to stay away from the blazing walls in case they collapsed. But she also had to get her story.

Rosie started to interview the people who were out on the street, shivering in their bathrobes and wrapped up in the commotion. Rosie began by asking the five W's: who, what, where, when and why. She worked quickly. People were cold and wanted to get inside. Rosie noted where the people lived and got their phone

numbers so she could call back for more information if necessary.

Rosie also talked to the firefighters. She asked how fierce the fire was — three alarms? Were trucks called from other communities? Had anyone been injured?

By midnight, Rosie was back home, entering the story in her computer. She didn't have to drive downtown to the newspaper office to deliver her story. She sent it from her home computer directly into the *Chronicle*'s computer.

Some editors and reporters rarely meet face-to-face, even though they work together for years — everything is sent via computer.

Rosie knew she might be called by an editor after the story was filed. Maybe she missed a bit of information or a sentence was unclear. But experienced reporters know what is needed for a good story and usually get it right the first time.

For Rosie, it was finally time to finish her pizza and find out "who done it" in the video.

100 years ago...

Reporters like Rosie can find themselves in potentially dangerous places when out on assignment. Ida Wells Barnett (1862–1931) investigated and wrote about the treatment of African Americans long before the civil rights movement of the 1960s. She witnessed violent confrontations, and her reports brought the story to thousands of readers.

Roaming reporter "Stroller" White (1859–1930) also found himself surrounded by danger when he wrote about the colorful events and characters of the Klondike Gold Rush, just before 1900.

A picture is worth...

Many times the reason you stop to read an article is because the picture that goes with it grabs your attention. Picture editors are always on the lookout for photographs that will make stories more dynamic.

After he assigned Rosie to the fire story, the *Chronicle's* editor called photographer Max Henry. Max grabbed his cameras and raced to the pickle factory. Max took hundreds of pictures to get one great one that would go with Rosie's story.

Photographers, like reporters, can sometimes find themselves in dangerous situations. To get an extraordinary shot from just the right angle, Max might have to climb a tree, scale a wall, crawl along the ground or stand on top of his car. He's always looking for that special something that will make his picture tell a story. Max felt he got a great shot at the factory fire — a firefighter silhouetted against the glowing flames.

The picture editor agreed that the photo was outstanding, but this doesn't always happen. Sometimes the picture editor doesn't agree with Max and selects another photo. After a photo is selected, it is cropped (trimmed) to focus on the most important or dramatic part. Pictures can also come from the *Chronicle's* library or from a wire service (see the next page).

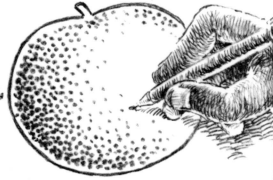

130 years ago...

Photographers throughout history have been in dangerous situations and yet have managed to capture powerful pictures of important events.

Mathew Brady (1823–1896) changed the world's view of war when he photographed Civil War battlefields in the 1860s. The photos were taken and developed right on the field, sometimes even while the battle was going on. Like other photographers, Brady carried all his darkroom equipment with him in a covered wagon he called the "Whatsit Wagon."

SPOTS BEFORE YOUR EYES

Use a magnifying glass to look closely at a newspaper photograph. The picture is actually made up of thousands of tiny dots.

Draw the outline of an object, such as an apple, in pencil, *but* don't color it in. Instead, use a felt-tip pen to show the shading and contours by filling the apple with small dots. The shadowed areas will have the most dots; the light areas fewer. When you're done, carefully erase the drawn line around the apple, then tape your picture to a wall, step back and look at it. Your eyes will connect the dots and you will see a complete apple.

Tensions mount as regime takes over

VAPORA (AP) — Civilians in the war-torn province of Bathos are spending nights in shelters as their cities and villages are invaded by enemy troops from the neighboring province of Lagostina. The two provinces of Cloudenska are fighting over new boundaries established by the government three years ago.

Foreign news

Some large newspapers have foreign correspondents. These are reporters who live in foreign countries and send in reports when something newsworthy happens. The *Chronicle* can't afford to have reporters living all over the world. Instead, the newspaper uses wire services. These are news-gathering agencies that collect and distribute news to subscribing newspapers around the world.

The name "wire service" comes from the days when stories were sent over telegraph wires. Today, wire services send news stories directly through telephone lines into newsrooms around the world. At many newspapers, the wire services transmit directly into the paper's computer system.

Associated Press (AP), United Press International (UPI) and Reuters News Agency are wire services. They might have reporters stationed in Cloudenska. The *Chronicle* editors can choose which wire service report they wish to use.

CHOOSE A PHOTO

Wire services also provide newspapers with photographs. These are transmitted a bit like faxes. In the newsroom, a selection of photographs flashes onto a computer screen. An editor selects a photo from this "picture menu," presses a button and in minutes the photo is copied and ready to be processed for the *Chronicle*'s pages.

Suppose *you* were the editor responsible for the Cloudenska story. Which of these photos would you choose? Try writing a caption (a sentence describing what is going on in the picture) for the photograph you've chosen.

Robins clobbered by Duets! Ouch!

by **Tommy Lau**
CLAIRVILLE CHRONICLE

Say it ain't so. The Robins were asleep at the bat during the last game of the Continental League playoffs this year. Balls were lobbed over the heads of third basemen.

Banners that were waved so proudly a few weeks ago made good hankies to wipe away the tears of disappointment in the stands. When it was all over, the Duets had clobbered the Robins by a score of 12 to 1.

Sports and entertainment

Sports reporter Tommy Lau usually has great fun on his assignments, but playoffs mean more work! He has to collect the facts, like any other reporter, but he also gets to use some of the most colorful language in the newspaper. Words like *clobbered, sucker-punched* and *slam-dunked*.

Years ago, sports reporters sat through a game and took notes. If the game was over at 11 p.m., they hurried to the newspaper office and rushed to write an article for the midnight deadline.

When Tommy covered the Robins' game, he sat in the press box at the ballpark with his

lap-top computer. As the game progressed, Tommy wrote his story, play-by-play. By the time the Duets had clinched the title, Tommy's story was just about done. He just had to "top it up" (put on the finishing touches) and send his story via computer into the newspaper office.

Rocker Kinky L. Deeee wins fans with fun

by **Jesse M. Midha**
CLAIRVILLE CHRONICLE

The Texas rock sensation Kinky L. Deeee ("with four e's, if you please") is coming, and her fans are ready. Kinky's last concert here, in 1991, left people howling with laughter. How can you take someone seriously when she shows up on stage wearing a skirt covered with plastic toys and a shirt that spangles and shines more than Madonna's hippest corset?

Yes, Kinky's coming. Jasper Gale, stage manager at the Roxy, is already scrambling to assemble Kinky's list of dressing-room must-haves: a six-pack of exotic juice, a large bottle of antacid, a new issue of *People*, ten (and only ten) strings of red licorice, a pot of herbal tea and some extra safety pins to reattach toys that fall off during the show.

"Every artist sends us a very eccentric list," chuckles Gale.

Entertainment and sports stories cover events with lots of excitement and fun. The stories give readers relief from the serious and sometimes disturbing news around the world and help to educate them as consumers. Reviews of movies, concerts, books, ballets and plays help readers decide what to do, see and read.

275 years ago...

Benjamin Franklin (1706–1790) was a famous printer and newspaper publisher who became so successful he retired at age 42. He then began careers in science and government. Franklin's early success was the result of the training he received when he was a boy.

Long ago, boys as young as 12 could be apprenticed to printers. A contract was signed and the boy was trained to be a printer. But the boys were often treated as slaves; they had few freedoms, many chores, long hours and little food and clothing. Many apprentices, like Franklin, ran away from the drudgery and set up their own businesses.

Today, people who want to become reporters or journalists don't have to become apprentices at a newspaper! Journalism students follow special programs at colleges or universities. There are plenty of opportunities to write all kinds of articles, and many fledgling reporters get to work temporarily at a *real* newspaper office.

The comics

Many people read the comics before they read any other part of the newspaper. Some readers are fiercely loyal to their favorite comic-strip characters. When a newspaper drops a strip, complaining letters may flood in.

Who and what are behind the comic strips in your newspaper? Meet Lynn Johnston, whose comic strip "For Better or For Worse" appears in more than 1500 newspapers around the world.

Q. Where do you get your ideas for the strip?

A. I'm on RECORD all the time, getting ideas. "Spot" ideas work well, like the image of a son talking on the phone all day but never saying a word to his mother. He's talked out!

Q. Do you create only the artwork?

A. Some cartoonists work with writers, but I do both the writing and the drawing. There's only a limited space for the message, and I am very demanding of myself. I write and rewrite the words for each strip. By the time I reach the last panel, I need a punch line or a pun or a strong remark.

Q. How do you draw the panels in your strip?

A. I use a template (a pattern) and draw the four panels on my board. Since my hands perspire a lot, I wear a cotton glove (with the fingers cut off) to keep the cartoon clean. In each panel, I sketch the drawings and print the words in pencil. Then I use ink and two different pens to write over the words and finish the picture. If I make a mistake in the drawing, I use white animation paint to cover it. When the paint is dry, I can draw over it. Sometimes I cut out a new panel and glue it over the one with the mistake.

Q. How far ahead do you work?

A. I work on the daily strips six weeks ahead of when they'll appear in the newspapers. The weekend colored strips are done eight weeks ahead. That means at Christmas, I'm already thinking about the Easter strips.

Cartoon quips

• Did you ever have a special blanket called your "security blanket"? The character Linus in the comic strip "Peanuts" gave us the expression. His blanket went everywhere with him and made him feel safe and secure.

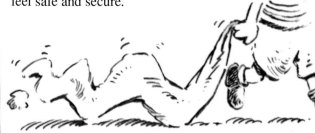

• Comic strips are full of *onomatopoeia*, or words that sound like what they're describing.

• Look on the opinion-editorial pages of a newspaper (see page 18). Is there a cartoon about a major event in the news? This editorial cartoon often contains a caricature (a funny portrait) of a famous news-maker.

Q. We hear about "writer's block." Is there such a thing as "cartoonist's block"?

A. There are dry times when I have no ideas. It's good that I'm always working so far ahead on the strip, just in case it happens. Sometimes I stop working and take a long walk. Or I read something funny to get in a good mood. Even sleep can help. Sleep can be part of the creative process.

Q. Can you offer any tips to young people who would like to become comic-strip artists?

A. Practice a lot. Copying isn't bad unless you say someone else's work is yours. Be honest. Develop your own style. A cartoonist's style is as personal as his or her signature. It takes a long time to get both the way you want them. Learn from others. I learned a lot from my favorites, like the artists in *Mad* magazine. And never say, "I'm good." Say, "I could be better."

For Better or For Worse

© Lynn Johnston Productions Inc.

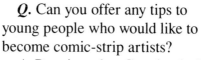

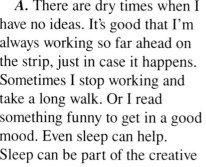

100 years ago...

Joseph Pulitzer was first to print the Sunday comics in color in his New York newspaper, the *World*. He hoped colored comics would boost his newspaper's sales.

One of the comic strips was about life in the poorer sections of a big city. It featured a boy called the Yellow Kid, dressed in a baggy, yellow smock. The comic strip was an instant success.

Pulitzer's rival, William Randolph Hearst, bought out the *World* supplement and added it to his paper, the *Journal*. Pulitzer hired someone to create another Yellow Kid, and the competition between the newspapers escalated. The Kid became the symbol of the battle between Hearst and Pulitzer as each tried to outdo the other to get more readers. Crime stories, scandals, rumors and invented news filled the pages of both papers. Soon this kind of reporting was known as "yellow journalism" because each paper was famous for the Yellow Kid.

The one New York paper that did not join the yellow war was the *New York Times*, and it is the only paper of the three to survive until today.

Joseph Pulitzer (1847–1911) remains a news-maker every spring when newspapers announce the names of the Pulitzer Prize winners. These awards are given to writers who excel in the fields of journalism, literature and music. Pulitzer's will established the prize and funded one of the first North American schools of journalism at Columbia University in New York.

Op-Ed

The Op-Ed (opinion-editorial) pages are the center of opinion in most papers. On the Op-Ed pages, the editorial board of the *Clairville Chronicle* makes observations about events in the news. Large papers often print two editorials a day. A smaller community paper usually runs one editorial. These editorials are commentaries or observations about current events and government policies. Sometimes the editors use the space to praise someone, perhaps the winner of a peace prize, or to draw attention to the efforts of a hardworking but little-known organization.

Editorial cartoons are featured on the Op-Ed pages, too. They give the artist's viewpoint in pictures, not words.

The Op-Ed pages also carry Letters to the Editor, where readers write in to tell the *Chronicle* just what *they* think about local and world events. Sometimes people also speak out about the paper's treatment of the news.

Visit for the day

In the May 12 story "Students don't work hard any more," reporter Rosie Longo had the facts all wrong. Didn't she even try to talk to those of us who study hard every night, after we get home from evening part-time jobs? Where did she find these lazy kids? They're giving the rest of us a bad rep, and we think Rosie should give the other side.

We invite your reporter to visit us at Troy Harding School — she might like to follow us for a day or two and get the real picture!

DEVON SMILEY,
BLAIRE FRASER,
ANDREA NISBET,
ROBERT WOOD
and ten other students at
Troy Harding School

A paper's masthead is also found on the Op-Ed pages. The masthead contains business information about the paper, such as the name of the publisher, circulation figures (the number of people who buy the paper each day), the date the paper was established and the names of the Board of Directors. In some instances, the members of the editorial board are named.

Letters, editorials, masthead, artwork. Whew! That's a lot of information on just a page or two!

In my opinion…

Much of a newspaper deals with straight facts about people and events. But there's plenty of space for personal opinions, too.

Many newspapers have staff columnists, like Colin Spender (see below), who ponder the facts and then write their opinions. A columnist's views don't necessarily reflect the views of the newspaper or the publisher (the person responsible for the paper overall). A columnist can write about almost anything but usually has a specific area of expertise: city planning, women's issues, education, politics. Observations can be humorous, but they must not be libelous — that is, false statements written and published deliberately to damage a person's reputation.

THE CITY
by Colin Spender

Parks department is all wet

Have you heard the latest? Last Tuesday night's meeting in the Council Chambers did nothing to cool off the city's kids, but plenty to make the summer's heat even more unbearable.

"We're closing half of the city's public swimming pools," crowed Councillor Jim Smelter. "We've got to cut costs, save money," he added.

And this selfsame yo-yo proceeded to approve funds for jazzier park signs!

Who *cares* how trendy the signs are? People are out of work; lots of kids can't make it to camps, but they can cool off at the local pool. Maybe Mr. "Swelter" Smelter can offer up his in-ground backyard pool for the enjoyment of kids left standing sunbaked in the heat.

Freedom of the press

In many countries, people are guaranteed freedom of the press — the right to know what's going on. Reporters can write articles that are critical of their government without fear. But in some countries, there is no freedom of the press. The government suppresses information and sometimes even cuts out or blackens newspaper articles it finds offensive. This is censorship, or control of what people can read.

The people of Clairville are lucky. The *Chronicle* is not censored. Columnists like Colin Spender can speak out and disagree with public policies. The editorial board can criticize the government's actions. Even cartoonists can make social or political comments.

Special sections

There are many different sections in a newspaper. Some, such as Fashion or Food, only appear once a week. The editors of these special sections often choose a theme, then gather and assign articles that relate to this theme.

Chronicle Food editor Louise van Spinks has selected pizza as a theme for this week's Food section. Let's peek at her checklist for the section.

✓ Assign a reporter to research the origins of pizza. (Did Columbus eat pizza on the Santa Maria? If so, what kind?)

✓ Set up interviews with six Clairville chefs famous for their pizza. Ask for their recipes to print in the paper.

✓ Allow time for the Chronicle test kitchens to test the recipes. (Lemon slices on pizza!!!???)

✓ Report on taste test: invite ten students from a local school to choose their favourite pizza.

✓ Book photographer to snap the chefs' and students' photos.

✓ Check out local cooking schools with pizza-making courses.

✓ Arrange for illustrator to draw a great good-enough-to-eat pizza for the top of the page, and some trendy type to jazz up the final look.

Lots of planning goes into each special section of the paper, such as Sports, Business, Entertainment, Life and Travel. And some papers have *lots* of sections. Just ask a newspaper delivery person how much a weekend paper weighs — chances are he or she will say, "Too much!"

"Dear Ann..."
Some columnists answer questions sent to them by their readers. Ann Landers receives more than a thousand letters a week asking for information or sharing personal experiences.

Advertising

Newspapers are dedicated to keeping you up-to-date on the news. But the money you pay for your daily paper cannot keep a newspaper in business — it pays only a portion of the costs. The rest of the money needed to keep the paper going comes from advertising.

Advertisements, or ads, generate the funds needed to buy the ink and the paper, the computers and the office telephones. Ads provide money to pay the reporters, photographers, editors, printers and caretakers of the building. Each day's *Chronicle* has a different arrangement of ads, depending on how many businesses and people have bought ad space that day. Generally, newspapers allow for a certain percentage of ad space, available to the public for different fees,

depending on the size of the ad.

There are larger ads, like department-store or grocery-store full-page spreads, with drawings or photos. The Verblitz ad would be much smaller, and so would cost much less.

Some ads are designed by the business and others by the newspaper's designers or by advertising agencies. The finished artwork and text are placed throughout the paper, sometimes according to subject matter. For example, an ad announcing a sale at a clothing store would run in the Fashion section.

In the Classifieds section of the paper, you'll find paid ads for everything from used cars to house rentals to dogs for sale. People decide how long they want their ad to appear, and pay for it according to the newspaper's ad policy.

DESIGN AN AD

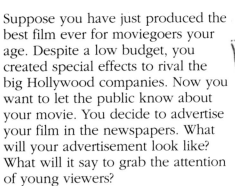

Suppose you have just produced the best film ever for moviegoers your age. Despite a low budget, you created special effects to rival the big Hollywood companies. Now you want to let the public know about your movie. You decide to advertise your film in the newspapers. What will your advertisement look like? What will it say to grab the attention of young viewers?

Design an ad and write some ad copy that "sells" your movie.

So you want a picture of Elvis for your mother's birthday, do you? Why not place an ad in the Classifieds of your local paper. Need an after-school job or a set of used roller-blades? Try the Classifieds.

WANTED: one velvet portrait of Elvis, "the King." Willing to pay $$$$. Ask for Art. 555-0000.

What if you have something to sell — your old bicycle, your old roller-blades, a velvet painting? Use the Classifieds to sell what you no longer need.

The cost of a classified ad depends on the number of lines of type or the number of words. So it makes sense to say what you want in as few words as possible.

Try writing one of these ads in as few words as you can.

• WANTED: VACATION RENTAL
Describe what you're looking for, when, where, and how much you're willing to pay.

• THE ULTIMATE YARD SALE
It's time to clean your closet and sell the items you've outgrown. Write an ad that will get you the cash you need for that vacation you want!

Personal information

The "hatched, matched and dispatched" columns announce births, marriages and deaths. Lots of information is packed into each notice.

If a world leader or famous movie star dies, the information will probably appear on the front page of the paper, or in the entertainment section. But there is usually a page set aside for birth and marriage announcements and death notices, or obituaries ("obits").

Try writing an obituary for a famous person from history. Maybe Cleopatra or Thomas Edison. Use a notice from your local paper as a model. Can you sum up a whole life in just a few lines?

What a Hat Trick!

SLAPSLOTZ — Deloris and Denver Slapslotz are the proud parents of their own little scorer, Sylvester, born on November 22 at Grace Hospital. Sly weighed in at 13 lbs. 6 oz. Many thanks to Doctor Marybeth Mackarony, goalie in attendance.

TOOLOOSE–MERTZ — Freida and Melwyn Mertz are pleased to announce the marriage of their daughter, Drusilla, to Mr. Tuckall Tooloose of Sneed, Alberta. The wedding took place at the Union Chapel in Auburn, Ontario, on June 10. All 20 of the bride's sisters were in attendance, handsomely dressed in black-and-orange feathered gowns. The couple spent their honeymoon in Paloma Sands National Park, where the avid birders caught sight of the rare fararee finch. Mr. and Mrs. Tooloose, owners of the Olde Birders' Shoppe, now reside in Clairville.

You be the judge

Newspapers often cover the same event but end up with very different stories. Imagine the circus has come to town. Three reporters, representing three newspapers, have been assigned to the story. Read the three clippings on the next page. Which one do you think is the best?

Propaganda

What you read in the newspaper is usually the first written record of what becomes history.

In some countries, newspapers can only report part of a story — usually the part that the government wants known. But even in countries where newspapers are free to publish any opinion they wish, newspaper owners may decide to publish only certain articles or opinions. In the past, newspaper owners sometimes played a role in history by carefully selecting what and how items were reported.

The systematic spreading of information to promote or damage a belief or cause is called propaganda. If a newspaper publishes propaganda, or selected news, it risks losing credibility. The best newspapers report the news as it happens — not as they want it to happen.

Angry demonstrators picket circus

by **Cal Green**
THE SALEM HERALD

…Members of the local Animal Safety League picketed the Summer Family Circus last night. A spokesperson demanded that the public not buy tickets for the remainder of the performances.

"It's awful," said Bill Jordano. "The animals are kept in small cages. Those tigers shouldn't be dancing in dry ice. They should be out in the jungle where they belong."

A close inspection of the cramped cages revealed that garbage had been swept into the corners and the animals were not receiving enough water during the recent heat spell …

Circus delights or abuses?

by **Mackenzie Chung**
THE BEVERLY TIMES

"…We always try to keep the animals as comfortable as possible," said Patsy Summer, co-owner of the Summer Family Circus. "As soon as we reach town, we're visited by members of the Animal Safety League, who check out the living conditions of the animals. It's difficult for us to maintain a spotless environment. We do our best."

When interviewed, animal rights supporters argued that they had seen unhealthy and dangerous conditions regarding the animals. The Safety League assured this reporter that they are carefully monitoring the situation and will close down the circus if necessary.

The Summer Family Circus takes pride in the fact that allegations of cruelty to animals have never been proven.

Summer Family Circus delights once again

by **Franny White**
THE MELROSE GAZETTE

…And what wonderful family entertainment! The colorful costumes, the lively music and the abundant talents of the performers made the afternoon fly by.

Three generations of the Summer family have performed in the circus. They train the animals, design the costumes and constantly change their aerial acts to attract families year after year.

The use of dry ice and special effects add to the drama of the show. The tiger act is simply magical …

Bravo, if you selected "Circus delights or abuses?" It gives the most balanced presentation of the news. Newspaper editors watch for a balance of viewpoints. A reporter's job is to report the news, not to make judgments. The Op-Ed pages, Letters to the Editor and columnists' pieces are the places for opinions.

2. Delivering the news

Do you have a paper route? Are there mornings when you don't want to get out of your warm bed to trudge through the cold, dark streets? You probably don't think about how the newspapers in your bundle got there. But all day, and even while you slept, the newspaper's staff worked hard to produce the newspapers for your customers.

Turn the page and follow the people at the *Clairville Chronicle* as they deliver the news.

160 years ago…
In the 1830s, New York publisher Benjamin Day gathered together about a thousand homeless boys from the city streets and offered them the chance to sell his paper, the *Sun*. The more papers they sold, the more money they made. They were the first newsboys, or "newsies."

Many of the boys were orphans. They were streetwise and fought over "owning" street corners, where they could sell lots of papers and make more money. Newsies were paid only a few cents, and most of their pay went back to Mr. Day. He rented them a bed and fed them for a fee.

Other newspapers soon discovered competitive kids could sell thousands of papers every day and hired as many boys, and girls, as they could.

11:00 a.m.
Meet and plan

It's a miserable, rainy Monday morning, and people are clutching mugs of steaming coffee as they enter the meeting room. It's time to organize the next day's morning edition of the *Chronicle*. Editors from the various departments of the newspaper sort through information and ideas, and decide what will go into the paper. There are hundreds of possible news items — and not enough space in the paper to print them all.

• The National editor finds out that the president will make an important speech about the economy.

• The City editor has just picked up a robbery on the police radio.

• The Foreign editor checks the wire service — a volcano is erupting in the South Pacific and lives may be lost.

The most important stories will get the most coverage. Editors debate which stories should make the front page. Some quick decisions have to be made. The more serious stories are called "hard" stories.

There'll be room for "soft" stories, too — the visit of Princess Zenobia, the 103rd birthday of Mrs. Elizabeth Hubbard and an interview with a parrot who reportedly can speak 500 words. And what's new from the local theaters?

By the end of the morning meeting, the editors have a good idea of what will be going into Tuesday's paper. But more exciting stories can break during the next 12 hours!

GETTING IT DOWN

When reporters are covering a story, or interviewing someone, they may use speed writing to get the facts down quickly. Some reporters carry tape recorders, too, so they can double-check the facts later.

Let's say you found entertainment writer Jimmy Dean's notes for a Three Beets rock concert interview.

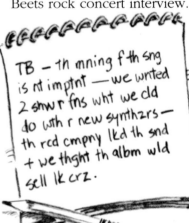

Can you "decode" Jimmy's notes? Hint: try adding some vowels. (The answer is on page 71.)

Noon
Who's on what?

The reporters and photographers are assigned their stories by the editors. Betty Esposito has been assigned the interview with the talking parrot. She sets up a time and place for the interview and starts jotting down questions to ask. What *will* she ask a parrot?

Betty will start with the five W's: who, what, where, when and why. *Who* is the bird — what's her name? *What* kind of bird is she? *Where* did she come from and where does she live now? *When* did she start talking and *why?* Betty will list as many questions as she can. She'll want to do some basic research on parrots. What will get a parrot talking? Maybe she should pack a treat for the bird. How long can she hold the bird's attention? Will she need to wear protective clothing?

With her bag packed full of crackers, pads of paper and, just in case, a leather glove, Betty is off to her interview.

Tracking a story
Marcel Benoit has been assigned to cover the robbery reported over the police radio. Neighbors spotted a man attempting to break into a house and called the police. When Marcel arrives on the street, he learns there's been a mix-up. The "thief" was Chief of Police Flanagan — the owner of the house! He'd lost his keys and had begun to pry the screen off a window so he could get inside. It takes awhile for all this jumble to get sorted out, and Marcel calls his editor to explain what's happened.

Marcel's editor tells him to forget the story and gives Marcel a new assignment. There's been a

roof cave-in at a suburban school.

"I'll send a photographer. You head out there fast!" the editor shouts.

Marcel jumps into his car. It's already 3 p.m. and the deadline looms.

3:30 p.m.
Back at the office

The rain has stopped. The editors are meeting again. Some stories have fallen through. New stories have come up. It's time for some major decision-making and maybe some raised voices.

The News editor is very anxious. Ten stories are competing for front-page coverage. There's only room for six. Marcel Benoit's editor rushes in with the news that the robbery was a nonstory.

"But I've got a roof cave-in at Hillside Elementary," he explains.

It's usually the News editor's job to make the final decision about what goes on the front page and what doesn't. He or she listens while the other editors try to "sell" their stories. Which ones will be chosen? What will best attract and inform the paper's readers? Articles are thrown out and more are selected.

The News editor wants a balance of local, national and international stories — and there are photographs to consider. The News editor makes the front-page selections — but the front page may still change.

CUT!

Newspaper photographers have been racing around town looking for great photos of important news stories. Here's a group of photos an editor might consider for the newspaper. *You* can be the editor! Choose the picture you think is the most dramatic. Cut a rectangle measuring 1⅝ inches by 2¼ inches out of the center of a sheet of paper. Use the cutout section to crop the picture you like.

Move the rectangular "frame" around until you've eliminated any distractions and have found the best part of the photo. The cropped photograph will have a lot more impact.

START THE TIMER...

Just when Minerva Montez thought her work was done for the day, her editor calls her over.

"Minerva," he says, "Dottie was writing a restaurant review and came down with stomach trouble. She's gone home. We have a hole on page 20, no filler reviews to put in, and guess who's going to write the story?"

He hands over Dottie's notes. Minerva has ten minutes to write the story. How well would you do in her place? Here are Dottie's notes. Set a kitchen timer for ten minutes and start writing!

When you've finished, write a short headline and put your name on the review — that's your *byline*.

Sunday p.m., Minnow's Cafe, Regent Street. Where all the kids hang out, blue walls, yellow cushions, slight smell of what?, chipped plate, had to ask for water, good salad, greens, usual veggies, funny waiter Gene, good jokes, seafood in cream sauce, parsley (I hate it), no fork on table, screaming kid in next booth, tables very close, fantastic coffee, dessert (apple pie) so-so, no wine served here, (do waiters deserve tips???), where's my coat, (feeling a bit woozy), waiter found out I was a reviewer, prices high, where are the kids who hang out?

CLAIRVILLE

NEW YORK

PARIS

SEOUL (NEXT MORNING)

The newsroom clocks show the time in different places around the world. Let's say a tidal wave devastates part of South Korea on Thursday afternoon. In South Korea, which is across the International Date Line, it's already Friday morning. Think about it: a newspaper can print tomorrow's news tonight!

6:00 p.m.
Fine-tuning the news

By dinnertime, the front page is ready. Since the afternoon meeting, there have been some changes; some of the stories the News editor selected have been bumped off the front page and moved to inside pages. Headlines and leads have been written. Headlines have to grab the reader's attention in a very few words: "Pretty Polly's a vocal bird," "Officials baffled by school cave-in." The lead is the opening to a story and summarizes the whole article.

Throughout the day, stories have been edited and fact-checked. Editors check for typos, misspellings, incorrect grammar and awkward sentences. They are on the lookout for anything that might cause legal problems for the newspaper. For example, a newspaper can't accuse a politician of being a thief without proof. Editors also read the stories to see if more information is needed and sometimes jazz up stories to make them more readable — all in an incredibly short time.

A fact-checker may contact story sources to double-check the information in an article. Does Polly speak 500 words, or is it 300? Is Flanagan spelled Flannaghan?

The wire services are checked over and over for late-breaking news that might mean changes for the front page yet again.

Editors decide how much space to fill with their choice of photographs, illustrations, graphs and maps. Finally, everything is ready to go to the composing room, where the bits and pieces are put together for printing.

The jobs of the editors and reporters are done. Tuesday morning's paper is taken care of, but they must begin to think about Wednesday's paper. Work on a newspaper never stops because the *news* never stops.

Designing the news

Throughout the day, articles, ads and photos are selected, edited and prepared for publication. As the material for a page comes together, that page is designed.

First, in the cut room, the ads are positioned on the blank pages. Once the ads are in place, the pages go back to the editors responsible for them. Now they know just how much space is left for articles and photos.

In many newspapers, everything is done on computers. The ad layout designer transmits the page with ads in position to the editor's computer. The editor inserts stories and headlines after the stories have been edited.

Next the pages (already put together) are sent by computer from the editorial floor to the composing room. With computer technology, some newspapers can compose the pages at their head office and then transmit photo images of the pages to a press building miles away to be printed. (In the near future, an editor will be able to send the image of a page directly from a computer terminal to the press, without any steps in between.)

When it's time to finalize the composition of the pages, the last pages of the newspaper are usually worked on first. The front page is left until the end, so that any important last-minute stories can be inserted just before printing.

9:00 p.m.
Getting ready to roll

Newspaper production constantly benefits from new technology. Not long ago, huge cameras photographed the page layouts, and the negatives of each page were developed in a small darkroom right next to the camera. Now the pages are received by computer as negatives.

These negatives are used to make the printing plates that will go on the press. Each negative is laid on top of the smooth, plastic-coated side of a metal plate. The negative-plate combination is placed in a machine that exposes the negative onto the plate. Another machine washes the plate and removes the unexposed material. (Soon negatives will be obsolete; the page design will be transferred directly onto the plate!)

The finished plate is no longer smooth. If you were to run your fingers over the plastic, you'd feel the bumpy texture of the letters, which are backwards, and the tiny dots of the photos. The finished plate is numbered and sent to the press room, where it will be attached to the press.

Lost weight
Metal printing plates once weighed about 45 pounds each. That was a heavy load for the pressroom workers to lift. The lead plates were melted down to make new plates. Modern plastic-and-aluminium plates weigh only a few ounces and are often recyclable.

News paper

Many historians believe that paper was invented in China 1800 years ago. This early paper was made of tree bark, hemp (a plant fiber), rags and fish net. These materials made paper that was strong and textured, and probably not very white.

Later, old clothes were recycled into paper. Dealers called out in the streets for rags and paid for them. The rags, usually made of linen, were cut into small pieces, washed and boiled with strong lye until the cloth disintegrated. Then the lye was washed away, and the remaining pulp, called "stuff," was used to make paper. You can still hear people talk about the "rag content" in paper.

Because millions of newspapers are printed around the world every day, a cheaper paper was needed. Called *newsprint*, it is made from various wood products and recycled paper. Water is an important ingredient in the manufacture of newsprint. As the newsprint goes through the press, special misting machines add moisture to the press room's atmosphere to help reduce the paper dust that is produced during the printing process.

130 years ago...

In 1863, the Civil War was raging in the United States and newsprint was scarce. But the *Daily Citizen* of Vicksburg, Mississippi, didn't let the paper shortage stop production. Unused rolls of wallpaper were collected from citizens, and the newspaper was printed on the back of the wallpaper.

150 years ago...

If you lived in Paris, France, in the 1800s, you might have found yourself reading a bedsheet newspaper, so called because it was huge — almost as big as a sheet.

9:30 p.m.
Start the presses!

The pressroom at the *Chronicle* is an im-*press*-ive room about three stories high. Narrow metal stairs, catwalks and bridges surround the machinery. Footsteps clang on the metal walkways, the overhead misting machines softly hiss and the voices of the people running the press rise and fall. Later, when it's time to "roll the presses," the noise will be deafening.

On the floor below the presses are huge rolls of newsprint, some as tall as an adult. As a roll is needed, it is moved into place beneath a press and fed into the machine. The metal printing plates are fixed onto the press and, with a flick of a switch, the paper begins moving through the press in one long sheet at a speed of about 20 miles per hour.

The printing presses not only print; they also fold and cut the newspapers. The paper is a blur as it moves through the press. Each section of the paper is printed separately; then all the sections meet at the folding machine. The newspapers come off the press with each section in its proper place. Thousands of papers can be printed in one minute. The presses are so noisy that workers have to wear earplugs. Some wear headsets and listen to music.

Some large newspapers, like the *Clairville Chronicle*, print more than one edition a night. The *Chronicle* prints at 9:30, 10:30 and midnight. Sometimes there are only slight changes from one edition to the next. But if an important story breaks, there may be a whole new front page. An editor is usually on hand to deal with any changes. The press can be stopped quickly if major changes are to be made, but such stops can be expensive.

Future news: robot express?

A newspaper run by robots? Well, not quite. But some large newspapers, like the *Toronto Star* and the *Los Angeles Times*, are already using Automatic Guided Vehicles (AGVs) to position huge, heavy rolls of newsprint onto their presses. These computerized robots are guided by wires embedded in the floor and travel at walking speed. AGVs are also used in mailrooms to move heavy loads of finished newspaper bundles. In the future, robots will no doubt have many more chores to do at the printing plant.

500 years ago...

Imagine writing an entire newspaper out by hand. By the time you finished, the news would be old. To speed up the process, printing presses were developed.

German printer Johann Gutenberg (1400–1468) invented movable metal letters (type) and is called the "Father of Printing." He adapted a winepress to make what is called a flatbed printing press.

In Gutenberg's shop, the pages of type were held in place in a "form," and the form was placed on the "bed" of the printing press. Ink was dabbed on the type, and paper was then placed on top of the page. A heavy plate was then screwed down tightly onto the type so that the ink was transferred from the type to the paper. After the sheet of paper was printed, it was removed to dry. The type was re-inked and the process continued. It took a long time to complete a printing job this way.

7:00 a.m.
Tuesday morning

The news that started its journey at the editors' meeting on Monday has finally arrived for newspaper deliverers, or "newsies," to distribute. When Lindsay Brian does her paper route, she joins a long line of newsies stretching back through more than 100 years of history.

Today, many newspapers still hire boys and girls to deliver papers. But in some communities, parents worry about safety, or kids are too busy for paper routes. So sometimes an adult newsy driving a car filled with newspapers breaks the morning silence, as the *Chronicle* lands on the front porch with a THUNK.

Hot off the press!
Have you ever wondered what "hot off the press" means? Printing presses move at great speeds, and the friction created heats up the paper as it whizzes by. A newspaper comes off the press as warm as toast, the aroma of the ink wafting in the air. So the newspaper is actually hot.

A real newsboy's story

Young Joseph Granfield was a newspaper delivery boy in Boston in the 1930s. If you have a paper route, you can see just how much has changed for newsies.

I started delivering papers during the Depression, when I was 12 years old. I walked 2 miles to the paper shack, an old garage where the papers were bundled for us to deliver. Max was the young man in charge; he put the papers in piles.

The boys had to count the piles twice to make sure they had the right number. If a boy was short papers on his route, he had to pay for them himself.

I started delivering at 6 a.m. each weekday and finished my route in time for school at 8 a.m. I also delivered papers again after school and on weekends.

A paper was 12 cents a week, plus one cent for delivery. I had the longest route — 152 papers each day — so in a good week I made $1.50. But this was the Depression, so a lot of people couldn't pay, and sometimes I worked the whole week for nothing.

The papers were bundled flat and tied with a strap. During the week, I carried all 152 papers under my arms. On Sundays, the papers were bigger, so we used two-wheel wooden carts to pull the papers along our routes. Only the main streets were paved, so the wheels got stuck in the mud.

It was an ordeal doing the route. In the winter, I wore a long woollen coat. Halfway along my route, I delivered a paper to a drugstore owner. There was a wood stove in the one-room store, and I would take off my coat to get warm. The coat was so stiff with ice that it stood by itself in the middle of the room. The druggist got angry because the puddle from the melting ice spread over his floor! Then it was time to put my coat back on and finish my route.

I also sold papers on the trolley-car route, but only on *my* section of the route. My territory for selling went as far as the trolley-car house. There were other boys selling papers at the house, and we called them the "Car House Rats." We had to watch out because some of these boys were bullies, and there were scuffles to protect our own routes.

Only the poorer boys had routes, because our families needed the money. It was all work and no fun. But when I was in high school, I used my long route up and down hills to help me train for the city track championships, and I won two major races.

Half of my earnings went to my family for food. It was the same for other boys, too. Girls didn't deliver papers then — they stayed home and helped their mothers around the house. In some families brothers had different routes; this gave the family some income.

Usually, the other half of my money was spent on something I needed, like a sweater. But I managed to buy a brand-new balloon-tire bicycle, and that was like buying a new car! It took me two years to save the $27.00 I needed for the bike. It was my first bicycle, and nearly 60 years later I still have it.

3. Publishing your own newspaper

A newspaper is like a pizza. It has the same crust (the various departments), but the toppings (the stories) change, giving the paper a different flavor each day.

What goes onto a pizza crust depends on who orders it. The same is true for newspapers. Try combining pineapple (travel), ham (comics) or hot peppers (sizzling photos). How about mushrooms (underground news) and green peppers (gardening)? Add some spice (gossip) and, before you know it, you have a newspaper your readers will devour.

Ready to cook up your own newspaper? Follow the nine easy steps in this chapter.

1. Pick an audience ... and a name

Before you can publish your paper, you need to know who it's for. Kids in your class or school? Members of a stamp, fan or other club? Your family? Once you've decided on your audience, you can choose a name.

When he's not Superman, Clark Kent is a mild-mannered reporter for the *Daily Planet*. Comic-book heroine Brenda Starr works for the *Flash*. Many newspaper names describe ways of announcing something:

• the *Clarion* — a trumpet that's loud and clear
• the *Gazette* — an announcement or report
• the *Herald* — a crier or messenger of important news
• the *Chronicle* — a record of historical events.

Other papers use names that recall parts of our huge universe, the source of all news — the *Globe*, the *Mercury*, the *Star*, the *Sun*, *Le Soleil*.

What will you name your newspaper? Here are some tips:

• Keep the name short. You'll want it to appear very large at the top of the front page.

• If you're publishing a club paper, choose a name that reflects your group's goals. Maybe *Pawprints* for an endangered species club paper? For a family newspaper, how about a name that plays on your family's name? For example, "Johnston" once meant someone from "John's Town" — call your paper the *John's Town Crier*.

2. Create a "look"

Your paper has a name — now it needs a "look."

Newspapers come in all shapes and sizes. Since you'll want to photocopy your paper, the easiest format is 8½ inches by 11 inches. If your copier prints on different sizes of paper, you may want to use 11-inch by 17-inch sheets instead.

How many columns of type will your newspaper have? The *Chronicle* (see page 43) has six columns. For a smaller format, you might want to try two or three columns — or a combination of both.

Draw up a master layout sheet showing where the columns will go. Use a dark pen. Later, when you are ready to assemble your newspaper, you will place sheets of paper over this master layout sheet and use it as a guideline.

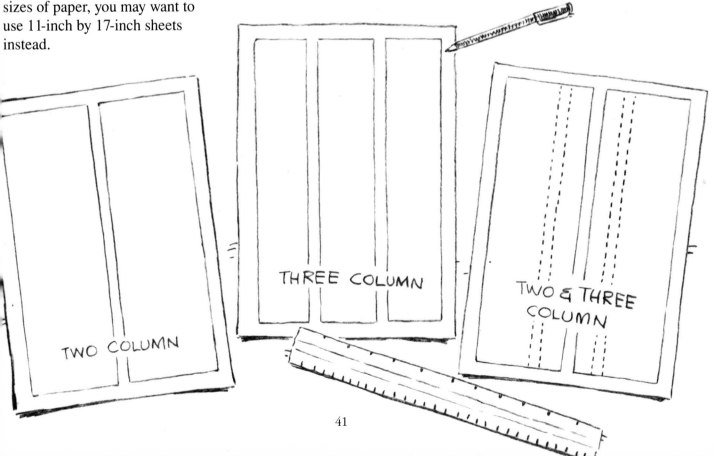

TWO COLUMN

THREE COLUMN

TWO & THREE COLUMN

Now you're ready to design your front page. The flag is the paper's name, which appears at the top of page 1. Use bold, attention-grabbing lettering for your newspaper's flag. Draw or stencil it. Visit a newsstand to get some ideas.

Experiment with different headline styles. You might use two or three different lettering styles. Try bold lettering for the hard news stories and finer lettering for other articles.

Visit for the day

TENSIONS MOUNT AS REGIME TAKES OVER

ROCKER KINKY L. DEEEE WINS FANS WITH FUN

Choose headings for the different sections (Sports, Entertainment, etc.). Have some fun with these.

SPORTS

And don't forget to design a masthead. Your readers will want to know who you are.

Front page puzzle

The *Chronicle's* front page is like a puzzle made up of many different pieces. You can use any or all of these pieces to make your paper look like a real newspaper.

A. *Ears* — The name of the paper is balanced by a brief weather report on one side and a guide to the paper on the other.

B. *Flag* — The name of the paper.

C. *Folio line* — The issue number, the day of the week, the date, the number of pages and the cost of the paper.

D. *Lead story* — Many newspapers print the lead story on the right side of the page. Some papers highlight the lead story with dark borders and place it elsewhere on the page.

E. *Byline* — The reporter's name.

F. *Off-lead* — A story second in prominence to the lead story.

G. *Play picture* — A photograph given a prominent position on the page.

H. *Caption* — A brief explanation of the photograph.

I. *Dateline* — Where a story is from.

If you look at other newspapers, you'll notice the puzzle pieces may be in different places. For example, an *ear* may have become part of an index (table of contents) in a lower corner. Each front page, including yours, will have its own design.

The Beacon St. Herald

Published at Beacon Street School, 15 Beacon Street, Clairville
Established 1993
Circulation 75

Wednesday, February 10, 1993
JENNIFER WONG/BRIAN SMILEY, Editors
JIM TENAKA/CONNIE LOPEZ, Writers
MICHAEL JEHAN/SARAH KING, Design
BRIDGET SHANNON, Photography

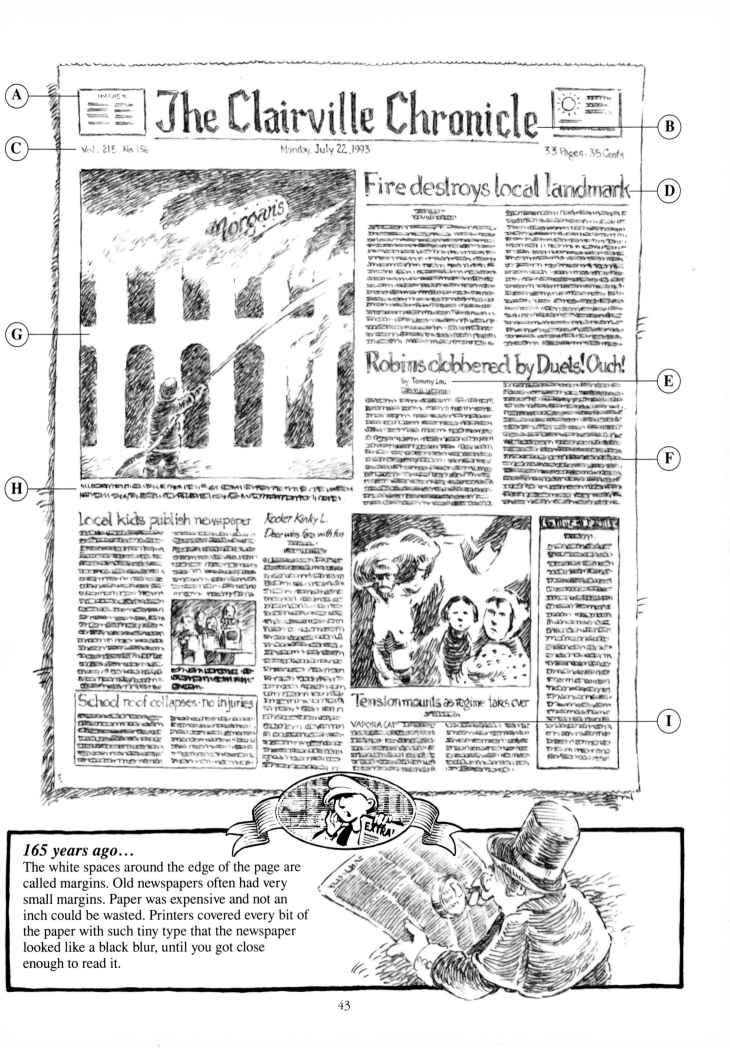

The Clairville Chronicle

Vol. 215. No. 156. Monday, July 22, 1993 33 Pages · 35 Cents

Fire destroys local landmark

Robins clobbered by Duels! Ouch!
by Tommy Lau

Local kids publish newspaper

Rooker Kinky L. Deee wins fans with fun

School roof collapses · no injuries

Tension mounts as regime takes over

165 years ago…
The white spaces around the edge of the page are called margins. Old newspapers often had very small margins. Paper was expensive and not an inch could be wasted. Printers covered every bit of the paper with such tiny type that the newspaper looked like a black blur, until you got close enough to read it.

3. Collect the news

You've got a name for your newspaper and a look. Now you need articles to fill the pages. For the front section — the first page or two — you might want to consider

• An interview with an interesting person. Perhaps Marion McSmudge, famous mystery writer for young people, is visiting the local bookstore or school. When did Ms. McSmudge decide to be a writer? How long does it take to write a book? Prepare some questions before you go to the interview. Use the five W's as a guide (see the next page).

• Reports of club, school or neighborhood events. Cover the annual fund-raiser for rain forest preservation, the election of officers for your student council or the personal appearance of your fan club's idol.

• Articles that give readers extra background information about a subject featured elsewhere in the paper. An article on threats to the rain forest will add to your fund-raiser coverage.

• A human-interest story — a shorter piece that gives readers a nice warm feeling. How did firefighters rescue a baby bear up a tree at the zoo?

You might want to include a photo with your story.

Why not add special sections containing some of these articles:

• An entertainment page filled with reviews of concerts, television programs, books and movies. How about a crossword puzzle or word search?

• A fashion page highlighting what's "in."

• An editorial page where the editors of your paper say what they think about the news. Once you've published several editions, you might want to include Letters to the Editor, giving readers a chance to comment on articles they have read.

• Sports reports on the latest wins and losses.

• Comics — see pages 16–17 for Lynn Johnston's advice.

• Classified ads where readers can buy and sell stuff.

Remember to think of your audience when you plan the sections of your newspaper. What do your readers want to know?

Kids make news

Many early newspapers employed copy boys to do odd jobs around the newsroom. They collected the wire news, got coffee for people and ran to the post office with the mail. When a young man turned 21, he could no longer be a copy boy. He might decide to become a reporter or pressman.

Today, boys and girls can still be copy kids — but their jobs are slightly different. They collect faxes, check on the wire services and the mail. You have to be at least 16 to be a copy kid, and you usually work nights and weekends. It's a great opportunity to learn about newspapers from the inside out.

4. Sell some ads

City papers sell space to advertisers. You may want to, too. After all, you'll have photocopying bills to pay.

Divide up your pages into units of a half-page, quarter-page and so on. Use your master layout sheet to fit the ads within the margins and column widths. Decide how much you will charge for various sizes of ads.

Local shops may already have an ad made up that you can photocopy. Or they may ask you to design one — for an extra fee, of course. If the advertiser has a business card, you can use it as the basis for your design. (Black-and-white cards reproduce better than color ones.) Or maybe there's a logo you can use. Write an attention-grabbing headline for the ad.

REMEMBER THE FIVE W'S?

The five W's — who, what, where, when and why — are the building blocks of newspaper articles. Many reporters start their stories by answering these questions. All the important information is in the first few lines of a story. Then the less important details are added. If there isn't enough space, the bottom part of the story can be cut without losing the important stuff. In newspaper lingo, this technique is called the Inverted Pyramid.

Check out the article below. Can you find the five W's? (The answers are on page 71.)

Singapore outlaws chewing gum

SINGAPORE (Reuters) — Singapore, unaffected by the weightier woes afflicting much of the world, has announced details of its New Year crusade — against chewing gum.

The environment ministry announced the ban Monday, citing the "perennial nuisance" of having to clean used gum from public places and subway trains. It said trains had been held up because of doors jammed by wads of gum.

A first conviction for import of chewing gum will carry a maximum fine of $7190, a year in jail or both.

Those convicted of selling gum can be fined up to $1426.

Tourists arriving in the island will have to declare chewing gum on customs documents when a government ban comes into force tomorrow.

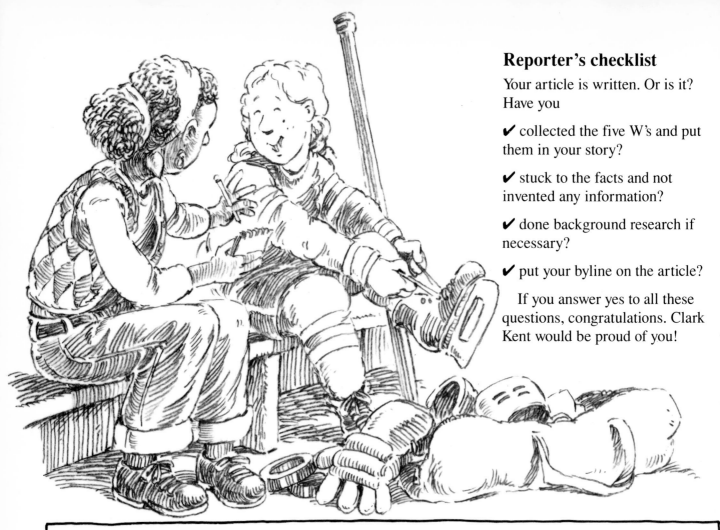

Reporter's checklist

Your article is written. Or is it? Have you

✔ collected the five W's and put them in your story?

✔ stuck to the facts and not invented any information?

✔ done background research if necessary?

✔ put your byline on the article?

If you answer yes to all these questions, congratulations. Clark Kent would be proud of you!

BACKWARDS WRITING

A headline, or "head," should capture the attention of readers and motivate them to read the article. Use punchy words for headlines — and keep them short.

Usually, the headline is written *after* you've written the article. But sometimes it's fun to try it the other way around. Can you come up with a short article to match these headlines? (By the way, these are *real* headlines from *real* newspapers.)

"Robber armed with cucumber"

"Tin can of soup kicking around after 135 years"

"200-year-old women's shoes found behind walls"

"Fishermen find feet in shark's belly"

"3 rare alligators found in paper bag"

5. Get the pictures

Newspaper pages would be ho-hum without photographs, drawings, cartoons and comic strips. These visuals add spice.

Invite friends who can draw to submit art that will make your newspaper's pages explode with action and humor.

• Some photocopiers can enlarge or reduce artwork to fit the columns of the layout sheet. Don't forget to crop pictures for maximum drama (see page 30 for cropping tips).

• Use photographs that have lots of black and white contrast. Gray areas won't photocopy well. If you don't have photos, don't worry. Draw all the cartoons, page decorations and portraits, like newspaper artists did long ago.

• Ask artists to draw their material with heavy black lines so the pictures will copy clearly.

47

6. Edit the stories

If someone tells you she's going to "blue-pencil" your article, it means that she will edit what you have written. Blue pencils were once used by editors to mark errors, suggestions and rearrangements in articles.

It can be discouraging to get an article back from an editor and see lots of changes. "I did my best work," you might say, "and look at what the editor did to it." That's when it's time to take a deep breath and remember that an editor is serving the readers and not you or herself. The editor is helping you put your best work on paper.

On your newspaper, reporters might try editing each other's articles.

ON YOUR MARK ...

Editors use special marks, like a code, to make changes and fix errors. The person who types or inputs the article into a computer knows what each mark means. If you're feeling really confident, try using these editing marks when you proofread your rough copy:

- **caret** (insert mark) — something has been added
  The editor may find out that ...

- **delete** — something is taken out
  Let's follow the staff of a city paper.

- **add a period**
  Later, the editor calls him

- **transpose** — exchange places
  ... wearing the traditional "newsboy's cap."

- **add a space**
  ... newspapers break the morning silence.

- **close up a space**
  ... newspapers break the morning silence.

- **add a comma**
  ... the editors reporters and photographers.

- **capitalize**
  When he's not superman, Clark Kent ...

- **do not capitalize**
  ... produce a special Newspaper.

- **start a new paragraph**
  ... stories already turned in. The front page editor ...

7. Type and proof

Once you've collected all the pieces of your newspaper — news articles, background features, columnists' pieces, editorials, interviews and so on — you're ready to type them up on a typewriter or computer. Set your margins so that they match the width of the columns on your master layout sheet. Type everything up. You'll end up with long columns of type called "galleys."

Sharpen your pencil and get ready to find any mistakes in the galleys. *Their's noting more irritatin then reading soemthing with a lot fo errrors init.* Mark all mistakes; then fix each one. If you're using a typewriter, use correcting fluid and type the correct item in the new white space. On a computer, make corrections and print out a clean, corrected galley.

250 years ago…

Long ago, every word in a newspaper was made by assembling individual letters. The letters, called "type," were backwards, so that when they were printed they would appear forwards.

The people who assembled the type were called typesetters. They had to be very skilled to compose words and sentences quickly with these backwards letters.

Our expression: "Mind your p's and q's" comes from a typesetter's problem. Because the letters were backwards, it was very easy to mix up the p's and q's. Typesetters had to pay strict attention to what they were doing — they had to mind their business! Other letters could be a problem, too. How about "minding your d's and b's"?

8. Page makeup

Now you're ready to make up, or lay out, your newspaper pages. Put a blank piece of paper over your master layout sheet. You should be able to see the lines from your master through it.

• Start with the front page. Place your flag, ears and other front-page elements where you want them. Leave room for an index. Don't glue anything down yet.

• Add your most important news stories — the ones that will grab a reader's attention. Don't forget to leave room for photos and headlines. Any article that is too long for the front page can be cut and continued on another page.

Carefully set aside the front page and move along to the other pages of your newspaper. One by one, fill them with ads, articles and visuals like photos, comics, etc. Think of your newspaper as a jigsaw puzzle. If a piece doesn't fit in one place, move it to another until all the pages are filled. You may need some "fillers" — jokes, free ads for good causes, silly stories — to fill holes in your layouts.

• When the entire newspaper has been laid out, glue the articles down. Put plenty of glue on the corners of articles. If they're not flat, the photocopier will make shadows on the finished newspaper page.

• Number the pages and compile an index. Remember you left space for it on the front page.

INDEX
Births 10
Books 8
Classifieds 9
Comics 7
Editorials 4
Letters 4
Sports 6

9. Print it!

You'll have to guess at how many copies to photocopy for your first newspaper. Reader responses will let you know whether to print more or fewer copies of the next issue.

Sort the photocopied pages in the right order and staple them together. (If you've printed your newspaper on large sheets of paper, fold them and fasten them together along the fold.)

The speedy delivery of your newspaper will ensure that your readers get the news while it's still "hot."

Congratulations!

You've worked hard on your newspaper. But newspaper editors and reporters can't just sit back and relax after one successful issue. The news is always happening. You have to get out there and chase it! Maybe that's why newspaper reporters are sometimes called newshounds. They have a nose for news and are always ready to dig up the details.

30
When "30" appears at the end of a reporter's story, it means "the end." Some authorities say "30" comes from the XXX symbol that early telegraphers used to indicate the end of a story that was sent by a reporter to a newspaper office. In Roman numerals, XXX is 30.

4. Recycling the news

Millions of people around the world read a newspaper every day. The next day they read a new newspaper. And so on, all year long. What happens to all the old newspapers?

Newspapers contribute piles of waste to our already filled dump sites. Paper is biodegradable, which means it breaks down and is absorbed back into the environment. But it takes a long time.

Staggering amounts of newsprint are used each day. A paper such as the *New York Times*, with a circulation of 1.2 million, uses 582 rolls of newsprint every night. Those paper rolls weigh as much as 118 adult elephants — and one of their babies!

Recycling newspapers can help. If newspapers are recycled, fewer papers will end up in landfills, and fewer trees will have to be cut down. Recycling decreases air pollution caused by burning the newspapers and can even create jobs in the recycling industry.

In the United States, the pulp-and-paper industry is already recycling massive amounts of wastepaper. Used newspapers can become shingles on your roof, insulation in your walls or the covering around the lead in your pencil.

Each of us has to help protect and nurture the environment and the Earth. It's a big job and a great deal of work. Let's make recycling part of our daily lives.

And don't forget — you can have lots of fun with used newspapers, too. Try a few of the activities in this chapter. You'll have fewer papers to put out for the garbage collector!

Recycled paper

Here's how to make new paper out of old news. This paper will be grayish because of the newspaper, but the texture will be interesting when grass or tiny leaves are added. If you add herbs, such as lavender, you'll have scented paper. A box of handmade paper makes a wonderful gift.

You'll need

newspaper cut into small pieces
other materials, such as bits of
    used envelopes (for whiteness),
    dried grass or vegetable
    peelings (for texture), dried
    herbs (for scent)
a blender or food processor
warm water
a spoon
a dishpan
a piece of window screen smaller
    than the dishpan
paper towels
sheets of newspaper
a rolling pin

1. Put a handful of newspaper pieces and bits of the other materials into the blender. Be careful not to overfill the blender — half-full is fine. Add warm water, one spoonful at a time, and blend the materials into a mushy pulp. (The pulp shouldn't be runny.)

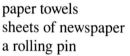

2. Pour the pulp into the dishpan. Make more pulp until the bottom of the dishpan is covered with a thin layer.

3. Add warm water to fill the dishpan more than halfway. Stir.

4. Hold the screen with both hands and slowly lower it into the dishpan.

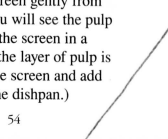

5. Shake the screen gently from side to side. You will see the pulp begin to cover the screen in a thick layer. (If the layer of pulp is thin, remove the screen and add more pulp to the dishpan.)

6. In one motion, lift the screen up and out of the pan.

7. Let the excess water drip into the pan. (If the layer of pulp is still thin, scrape off the pulp and repeat the dipping process.)

8. Lay the paper towels out on newspaper sheets. Quickly flip the screen upside down onto the paper towels. Tap the screen so that the pulp falls onto the towels.

9. Cover the pulp with another towel and use the rolling pin to roll excess water from the new piece of paper.

10. Lay the new paper flat on sheets of newspaper and let it dry overnight. (To dry the paper quickly, ask an adult to help you iron the moisture out of it. First, cover the paper with a large sheet of absorbent scrap paper; then quickly iron it. When the pulp stops "steaming," the paper is dry. But be careful — too much heat and the paper will burn.)

You are invited to a birtha... Date: J

Yesterday's newspaper

Paper isn't the only leftover when you throw out a newspaper. What about all the ink? During the recycling process, the ink is removed. For every 1000 tons of recycled newspapers, about 200 tons of sludge — including old ink — are left behind. This sludge isn't toxic, so it can be reused. For example, some sludge is used as mulch on farms. This mulch is a protective covering that keeps moisture for plants, protects their roots from freezing and controls weeds.

People are looking for new ways to recycle every bit of your daily newspaper. Some Japanese farmers have come up with an unusual idea. Along with their regular feed, Japanese farmers are feeding their cows old newspapers mixed with molasses. This "newsy" meal is cheaper than hay, and the milk production of the cows is high. Scientists have discovered that ingredients in the newsprint have more protein than dried beef, soybean meal or skimmed-milk powder. They hope that one day newspapers may help the world's food supply problems.

Wrapping paper

With a little bit of paint and a few recycled objects found around the house, you can make one-of-a-kind paper for gift wrapping. You can also use the paper to cover books and boxes (good for collections) and to tidy up school folders. For an extra-special look, try gold, silver or Day-Glo paints, and add glitter while the paint's still wet for some shine! All of these ideas start with a large sheet of newspaper.

1. *Splatter paper* — Dip an old toothbrush into water and tap off the excess. Then rub the brush into some watercolor paint. Hold the toothbrush over the sheet of newspaper and rub *up* the brush with a craft stick or old pencil. Voilà! Dotted paper! (Watch out! If you rub *down* the brush, *you'll* be the dotted end product.)

2. *Sponge printing* — Lightly dip a piece of sponge into paint and blot it onto a sheet of newspaper. Try adding several layers of color for a rainbow effect.

3. *Potato printing* — Cut a potato in half and wipe the surface dry with a paper towel. Mark a design on the surface; then cut away the parts of the potato that you *don't* want to print. A quick dip into a bit of paint and you're on the way to imaginative wrapping paper.

4. *Good impressions* — Dip corks, buttons, caps from bottles and other objects into paint and press them onto a sheet of newspaper. Think patterns!

5. *Stenciling* — Draw a design you like on a sturdy piece of cardboard. Let's say it's a tree. Cut out the tree and leave the rest of the cardboard intact. Lay the tree stencil on a sheet of newspaper and either splatter (see number 1) or sponge paint (see number 2) over the cutout part of the stencil. You can cut more stencils and add them in layers. Maybe you'll end up with a forest of pines!

6. *Combing* — Long ago, settlers decorated furniture, walls and everyday items with paint and a comb. Brush paint in a thick layer on a sheet of newspaper and then run an old comb through the paint before it dries. Change directions, wiggle the comb while you pull it across the paper or make waves. Experiment and add another color. Comb the two colors together.

7. *Fast wrap* — Use the colored comics from the weekend papers for an instant gift wrap. Foreign-language papers also look interesting when wrapped around a box and polished off with a huge, colorful bow.

Odor eaters, bug beaters and super cleaners

The ink and chemicals in old newspapers make them powerful helpers around the house.

• To ripen bananas quickly, wrap them in newspaper. The bananas won't ripen before your eyes, but they will be ready the next day, thanks to chemicals in the paper. Some farmers mound shredded paper, mixed with straw, around field vegetables to help them ripen quickly.

• To get the smells out of a used glass jar, put crumpled newspaper in it and seal the jar for a few days. The jar will be odor-free when you open it because the newspaper absorbs the old smells. The jar is ready to recycle.

• Next winter, wet boots won't make you hold your nose if you stuff them with crushed newspaper and let them dry naturally. The boots will also keep their shape.

• Shred old newspapers to line the cat's litter box or the gerbil's cage. Your pet — and your nose — will thank you.

• Moths don't like the chemicals or the ink in a newspaper, so put some old newspapers into the boxes or drawers with your out-of-season clothes.

• Newspaper torn into small bits makes great mulch for your garden. The newspaper adds to the soil's organic content — and keeps harmful insects from snacking on your crops.

• The next time you help wash windows or silver, try using newspaper instead of paper towels to rub your cleaner on and off. There'll be fewer streaks and more shine when you're finished, thanks to the inks and paper. Recycling newspapers in this way saves paper towels, too.

Astound-ink!

Fill a swimming pool with ink and you'd have enough ink to print almost two million newspapers.

De-inker

Do your fingers get inky after you read a newspaper? Long ago, ink was made from berries found in the wild. Then printers developed inks made from petroleum (oil) products. The first oil-based inks were very black — and very easily smudged. People sometimes wore dark gloves or special paper cuffs to keep clean while they read the paper.

In the 1980s, new inks made from soya beans were developed. Yes, ink made from soya beans! These soya inks smudge very little and are easier to remove from the newsprint when it's time to recycle.

Papier-mâché

The ancient Chinese molded mashed-up paper mixed with water into bowls and other household items. You can do the same thing with strips of old newspaper. Papier-mâché is French for "chewed paper."

Here are four papier-mâché ideas to get you going. Once you've got the hang of it, let your imagination go wild. What about

a papier-mâché tray or stool? The Chinese and Europeans of long ago filled their homes with marvelous papier-mâché items — like desks!

Papier-mâché paste

Here's the basic recipe for papier-mâché paste.

You'll need
all-purpose flour
warm water
a large bowl or bucket

Mix the flour and water together in a large bowl or bucket until you have a paste that feels like porridge — the gloppier the better.

Papier-mâché bracelet

You can make an armful of bracelets or enlarge the design and make a crown to top off a wonderful costume.

You'll need
newspaper (sheets and strips)
tape
papier-mâché paste (see above)
an empty soda bottle
acrylic or poster paints
bits of broken jewelry (optional)

1. Cut a piece of newspaper long enough to go around your wrist (allow extra, too). Fold the piece

of newspaper in half lengthwise, and tape the ends together to form the circular base of your bracelet. Try it on and make sure it slides over your hand easily. Your finished bracelet will have a layer of papier-mâché covering it. Adjust the size of the bracelet so that it fits you *and* leaves room for the papier-mâché.

2. Dip the paper strips into the paste, remove the excess glue and wrap the strips around the base until the bracelet is pleasingly plump.

3. Hang the bracelet over the neck of a soda bottle to dry.

4. When the bracelet is completely dry (usually after 24 hours), get out the paints and be creative. You may want to recycle broken jewelry and glue on beads and chains. If you've made a crown, glue on feathers and huge gems.

Papier-mâché bowl

You'll need
a small glass bowl
petroleum jelly
newspaper strips
papier-mâché paste (see page 58)
scissors
acrylic or poster paints
clear plastic spray (optional)

1. Smear the outside of a small glass bowl with petroleum jelly. The jelly will keep the papier-mâché from sticking to the bowl and will make it easier to remove.

2. Dip strips of newspaper into the bucket of flour and water paste and run the strip through your fingers to remove the excess paste. (Wear a smock — this is messy work!)

3. Lay the strips one at a time over the bowl, crisscrossing the strips and overlapping them until the entire bowl is covered with wet newspaper. Use six or seven layers of paper.

4. Set the bowl aside in a dry place and let it air dry for at least 24 hours. (It may take longer, depending on how thick the paper layers make the bowl.)

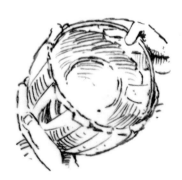

5. When the papier-mâché bowl is completely dry, carefully remove it from the glass-bowl mold.

6. Use scissors to trim the edge of the bowl to give it a neat line.

7. Use acrylic or poster paints to decorate your papier-mâché bowl.

8. When the paint is dry, you can spray the bowl with a clear plastic spray to make it more durable. You can also use the bowl as it is, for dry items only. Do not get papier-mâché items wet or the paper will become pulp again!

A party piñata

In Mexico, papier-mâché piñatas are stuffed with candies and smashed open on special occasions, such as birthdays. Make your own piñata and fill it with treats — candies, pennies and coupons that say "I owe you ... " Include some tiny toys you no longer want. You'll be recycling them.

You'll need
a large balloon
thick string
bathroom-tissue tubes
newspaper strips
papier-mâché paste (see page 58)
paints, glitter, sequins, yarn, crêpe
  paper, tissue paper, buttons
tape

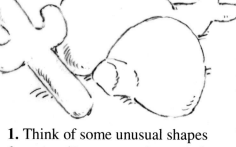

1. Think of some unusual shapes for your piñata — maybe a whale, an igloo or a cactus. Choose a balloon with the correct shape for the main part of your piñata. (For instance, a cactus will need a long, narrow balloon; a whale will use a rounder shape.)

2. Blow up and tie the balloon, and attach a loop of thick string where you want the top of the piñata to be. (This will be the loop to hang up the piñata.)

3. Cover the balloon with one or two layers of paste-covered newspaper strips.

4. If you want to add arms or legs to the main shape, attach the bathroom-tissue tubes (cut as shown) with the wet strips. Cover the tubes and the entire shape with more layers of papier-mâché. Don't worry if things get messy and don't look *exactly* like the real thing. Have fun!

5. After you've put on six or seven layers of paper, hang the piñata to dry and leave it for at least 24 hours.

6. When it's dry, punch a hole near the hanging loop and remove the balloon.

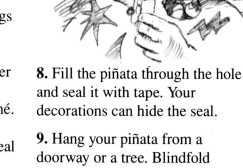

7. Paint your piñata with gusto. Add glitter, buttons, crêpe paper, tissue paper, sequins, yarn decorations or anything else from a scrap bag.

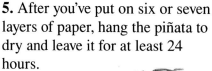

8. Fill the piñata through the hole and seal it with tape. Your decorations can hide the seal.

9. Hang your piñata from a doorway or a tree. Blindfold someone and hand her a broomstick. Then get ready to catch the treats.

> ### Where did the air go?
> When you cover a balloon with papier-mâché and leave it to dry, you'll get a surprise the next day. The balloon will be hanging loosely inside the piñata.
>
> The balloon isn't leaking. The wet paper and paste made the surface of the balloon cold. This caused the air inside the balloon to contract. The balloon lost volume and the surface began to shrivel. A bit of science in a piñata!

Life-sized sculptures

Once you've made smaller items out of papier-mâché, you can attack a larger project. Maybe you and your friends would like to make a life-sized statue of a character from a book. How about a self-portrait? You'll need *lots* of paste and strips, and something called an armature. The armature will support the weight of the papier-mâché covering.

You'll need

an old bucket

plaster of paris

a pole as tall as the figure you want to make (maybe an old hockey stick or broom handle)

smaller branches or poles to make arms, legs, etc.

string

heavy tape

a paper bag

plenty of papier-mâché paste, newspaper and paints

1. In the bucket, mix the plaster of paris with water, according to the instructions. Plant the long pole in the bucket of plaster of paris and let it dry.

2. For the arms, attach the crossbars (smaller branches or poles) with string and heavy tape.

3. To make a head, fill the paper bag with loose balls of newspaper and attach it to the figure with string or tape.

4. To flesh out your armature, wrap folded or balled newspapers around the arms, legs and body of the figure. Use tape or string to hold the newspaper in place.

5. Dip newspaper strips in the papier-mâché paste, remove the excess paste and cover the figure with six layers of papier-mâché.

6. Form features, such as a nose and ears, out of tiny balls of newspaper. A tissue can be scrunched up to make an eyebrow. Paper can be layered to make a mouth. Thick, messy layers can become hair.

7. Allow the figure to dry completely. Be patient. It could take at least 48 hours.

8. Paint the figure with acrylic, quick-drying paints — or dress it in *real* clothes! You can recycle yarn, jewelry and shoes on the sculpture.

Jacob's ladder

In the Bible, Jacob set out on a journey and traveled until the sun had set. Then he lay his head on a stone pillow and went to sleep. He dreamed of a ladder that reached from heaven to earth, and saw angels moving up and down it.

Capture the magic of Jacob's ladder with this newspaper toy. It will amaze your friends!

You'll need
newspaper
scissors
a ruler
tape

1. Stack six sheets of newspaper on top of one another. Cut a piece 12 inches wide and the full length of your newspaper. (Cut through all the layers.) Put the rest of the newspaper into the recycling bin — you won't need it for this activity.

2. Roll the layered piece of newspaper up loosely. Tape the roll shut.

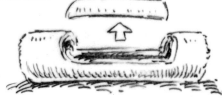

3. Cut the paper from the middle of the roll as shown.

4. Fold the two ends down.

5. Pull the top "rung" of the ladder, and the rest of the ladder will follow. Like the ladder in Jacob's dream, it grows higher and higher.

The fir tree

You've heard of making paper out of trees, but what about making a tree out of paper?

You'll need
newspaper
scissors
tape

1. Follow steps 1 and 2 for Jacob's ladder. Tape the roll at the bottom and the middle.

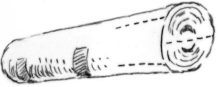

2. Cut down from the top three times as shown, with equal distance between each cut.

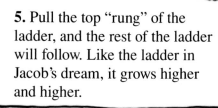

3. Fold the three sections down.

4. Hold on to the bottom of the roll and put your finger into the center of the roll. Pull the paper up from the center of the roll and watch your tree grow.

62

Made to last

You've won an incredible contest, and the local newspaper is featuring a story about you on the front page! If you want to preserve the article, try this recipe — it's supposed to keep the clipping for 200 years!

You'll need
1 milk-of-magnesia tablet (available at a drugstore)
a bowl
1 quart of soda water
a pan large enough to hold the clipping
paper towels
a table or other flat surface

1. Put the milk-of-magnesia tablet in the bowl. Add the soda water and let stand overnight.

2. The next day, pour the mixture into the pan.

3. Soak the clipping in the mixture for one hour; then remove the clipping and pat it dry with the paper towels. Lay the clipping on a flat surface and don't move it until it is completely dry.

Tricky strip

You can challenge your friends with this trick — and they'll be dumbfounded when they see the simple solution! You'll need lots of newspaper strips because no one will try just once.

You'll need
newspaper
scissors
a ruler

1. Cut the newspaper into strips about 9 inches long and 3 inches wide.

2. Give everyone a strip and then hold your strip up in the air.

3. Tell your audience to tear the strip down from the top, nearly to the bottom, in two places (as shown). Do not tear the strip all the way through.

4. Here's the challenge. Ask your audience to hold one end of the strip in each hand and rip it into three separate pieces *with just one pull.* Easier said than done!

5. Now show them how to do it. Fold the ripped strip in half as shown. Hold the fold in your left hand. Hold the two end pieces in your right hand. When you pull, the paper will end up in three separate pieces.

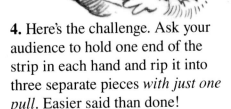

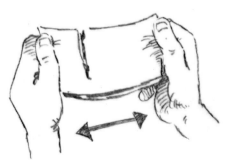

An optical delusion?

This neat trick can be done with a newspaper and some coins.

You'll need
newspaper
scissors
a ruler
a penny
a quarter
a table

1. Cut a 4-inch square of newspaper. (You might want to cut a spare in case your square tears while you're performing.)

2. In the center of the square, trace a penny and cut out the circle.

3. Show your audience that when you lay a penny on the newspaper square and tilt the paper, the coin slides to the center and falls through the hole.

4. Now challenge someone to drop a quarter through the *same* hole. Tell him he cannot tear the paper or touch the quarter with his fingers.

5. What's the solution? Put the paper flat on a table. Place the bottom edge of the quarter over the center of the hole. Then loosely fold the paper in half. Do *not* crease the fold.

6. Hold the paper up, loosely folded, so that part of the quarter hangs down through the hole.

7. Put one hand on each side of the paper near the fold. Slowly turn the sides upward and away from you. The quarter will drop through the penny-sized hole!

Newspaper relay race

Having a picnic or party with a bunch of friends? Divide the group into two or more teams, and give each team two sheets of newspaper. Use a rock to anchor another sheet of newspaper about 20 giant steps away. This will be the goal.

The object of the game is for all the team members to run to the goal and back, one after another, in a relay. But there's a catch. To move, a player must lay one of the sheets of paper down in front of her and step on it. Then she must lay the other sheet down, step onto it, turn around, pick up the first sheet and so on.

Each player must reach the goal in this way, before she can lift her papers and run with them back to her team. Once back at her team, she hands the papers to the next player. When all the players in a team have run, the team has finished — the first team to finish wins.

This game takes more coordination than you'd think. Just don't try to read the news while you're trying to run!

Musical newspapers?

Want to play musical chairs but can't find enough chairs? Why not use newspapers instead?

Lay sheets of newspaper about 3 feet apart on the floor or ground. Make an interesting-shaped path. While the music plays, everyone marches along the newspaper path, landing on a sheet of paper with each step. When the music stops, anyone not on the paper is "out." A sheet is removed from the path and the music begins again. Continue to play until only one person is left.

Or you can change the rules a little. When the music stops, anyone whose feet are *touching* the paper must drop out. Keep going until only one person is left.

Bricks

These bricks can be painted and used as building blocks. They can also be soaked in water and frozen to make ice bricks for picnic hampers. (An ice brick is also handy as an ice pack for injuries — just in case you get a black eye during the baseball game at the picnic!)

You'll need

newspapers
tape

1. Start with four sheets of newspaper. Fold the outside edges into the center fold as shown.

2. Fold the paper in half from the bottom up.

3. Repeat step 2 two more times.

4. Fold in half to the side as shown.

5. Make three more of these quarter-bricks by repeating steps 1 to 4 three times.

6. Insert the open end of one quarter-brick into the open end of another, and tape the sections together. You will have one half of a brick. Join two more sections together for another half-brick.

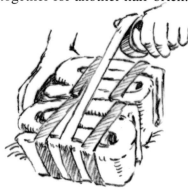

7. Finally, tape the two half-bricks together for the finished brick.

Now try to figure out how many layers of paper are in the brick. Hint: start counting at 500! (The answer is on page 71.)

(The answer is on page 71.)

Building sticks

Got a pile of old newspapers? Organize a building crew and roll some building sticks. Glue or tie the sticks together to make furniture. You can even make an indoor playhouse.

To make a stick, layer a few sheets of newspaper and roll them up diagonally from corner to corner. Tape the rolls closed and trim the ends to the length you want.

Paper cones

Have you ever bought bulk goods at the grocery store? Long ago, there were no packaged goods. When you went to the grocery store for cereal, sugar or candy, or to the bakery for buns, your purchases were handed to you in a paper cone called a scoop, or a twist.

In England, fish and chips traditionally have been served to customers in newspaper cones. The paper absorbs some of the grease and smells heavenly when salt and vinegar are added! Today, some fish-and-chip sellers use heavy waxed-paper containers that have been printed to look like — you guessed it — a newspaper!

You can make cones to use as a lunch bag, a popcorn package or a disposable trash bag for the car. The size of the cone depends on the size of the newspaper sheet you choose. Try a single sheet of paper folded in half for extra strength.

You'll need

a sheet of newspaper, folded in
    half
stapler or tape

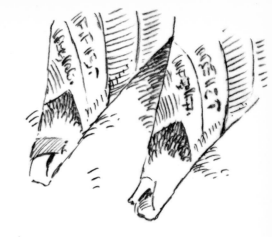

1. Turn your folded newspaper so the narrow ends are at the top and bottom, and the folded edge is on your left as shown.

2. Take the lower left corner and turn your hand under; the paper will form a cone.

3. Twist your hands a bit until you feel the cone tighten up.

4. Fold the bottom of the cone up and staple or tape it in place. You can also close the cone the way a grocer's assistant would have in 1904. Bend about 1 inch of the tip up from the bottom and fold it flat against the cone as shown. Make a sharp crease with your fingernail. Then bend about ½ inch of the cone down again, so the little point is aiming straight down. Crease that fold, too. The two creases will keep the bottom of the cone closed.

Fill the cone and fold the peak down over the top to close it up. Tape the peak down, and you've got a new package made of old news.

Beach umbrella

The next time you go to the beach, take along some newspaper, tape and a stapler, and you can make an umbrella to protect you from the sun. Pass your paper umbrella along to someone else when it's time to go home.

Handle — Layer five sheets of newspaper and roll them up diagonally. Tape the roll closed.

Stop — (The stop will keep your umbrella up.) Roll a sheet of newspaper diagonally into a tube strip about 2 inches wide. Roll a second sheet the same as the first. Staple the two tubes together at one end, and flatten them. Attach one end of this long flattened tube to the umbrella handle about 2 inches from the top. Wind the long strip around and around until you run out of strip. Tape the end down.

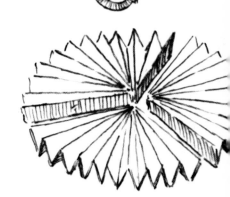

Umbrella top — Pleat two layers of newspaper like an accordion along their width. Fold the accordion in half. Make two more of these paper accordions. Staple the accordions together.

Assembly — Put the handle of the umbrella up through the center of the accordion top. The stop will keep the umbrella top from sliding down or closing. Tape the top to the handle to hold it in place.

Sonic snapper

All you need is some newspaper to fill a room with popping sounds. (Warning: the popping tears the newspaper, so make lots of snappers.)

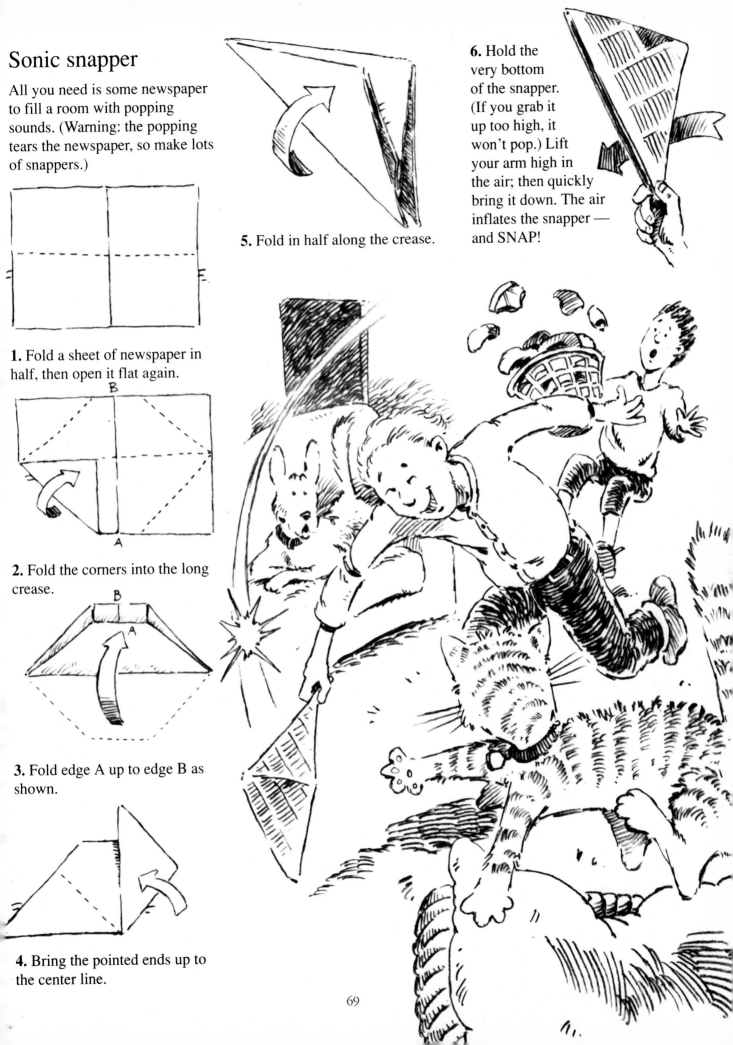

1. Fold a sheet of newspaper in half, then open it flat again.

2. Fold the corners into the long crease.

3. Fold edge A up to edge B as shown.

4. Bring the pointed ends up to the center line.

5. Fold in half along the crease.

6. Hold the very bottom of the snapper. (If you grab it up too high, it won't pop.) Lift your arm high in the air; then quickly bring it down. The air inflates the snapper — and SNAP!

Storyteller

Use your imagination when it's time to fill the inside of this newspaper storyteller with funny or totally outrageous fortunes for your friends to uncover!

You'll need

a sheet of newspaper
scissors
a ruler
a dark-colored marker

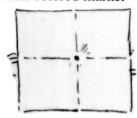

1. Cut a 9-inch square of newspaper. (Choose a part of the paper that is mostly type, not photos.) Make a center point by folding the square in half from left to right, then top to bottom.

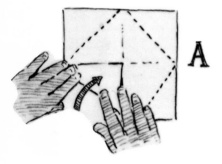

2. Fold the four corners of your square into the center as shown. This is side A.

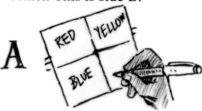

3. Turn the square over, and again fold the four corners into the center. This is side B.

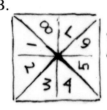

4. Turn back to side A. It now has four squares. Write the name of a different color on each square.

5. Turn to side B. It has eight triangles. Number each triangle, from 1 to 8.

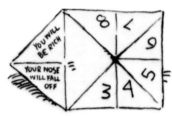

6. Lift the flaps on side B. There are eight triangle spaces to write funny messages, predictions or parts of a story. Fill each space with a different message.

7. Fold the flaps down again. Fold the storyteller in half and in half again. (These folds will make it easier for you to get your fingers in later.)

8. Now you're ready to use the storyteller. Gather your friends around. Fold the storyteller so you can slip the thumb and index finger of each hand into the "color" pockets on side A. Bring your thumbs and fingers together so you can easily move the pockets in and out.

Ask a friend to pick a color. She picks yellow. Move your fingers and the storyteller in and out, spelling y-e-l-l-o-w. Your friend then picks a number — 3. Count it out — 1-2-3 — as you move your fingers again. Finally, she chooses another number, let's say 4. You lift up the flap with the number 4 and read what it says underneath.

The more you use the storyteller, the more flexible it becomes. Try making a larger version with funny sentences under the flaps.

Answers

Getting it down, page 28
Three Beets — the meaning of the song is not important — we wanted to show our fans what we could do with our new synthesizers — the record company liked the sound and we thought the album would sell like crazy.

Remember the five W's?, page 45
Who — the environment ministry
What — a ban on chewing gum
Where — Singapore
When — Monday
Why — to solve the problem of gum in public places, including subway trains

Bricks, page 66
There are 512 layers of paper in each brick.

"A small town is a place where the news circulates before the newspaper does."
— Anonymous

Index